Elinor Gay

Skilful Susy, a Book of Fairs and Bazars

Elinor Gay

Skilful Susy, a Book of Fairs and Bazars

ISBN/EAN: 9783743344969

Manufactured in Europe, USA, Canada, Australia, Japa

Cover: Foto ©Andreas Hilbeck / pixelio.de

Manufactured and distributed by brebook publishing software
(www.brebook.com)

Elinor Gay

Skilful Susy, a Book of Fairs and Bazars

SKILFUL SUSY

A BOOK

FOR

FAIRS AND BAZARS

BY

ELINOR GAY

FUNK & WAGNALLS

NEW YORK
10-12 DEY STREET

1885

LONDON
44 FLEET STREET

PREFACE.

This little book is intended to lighten somewhat the labors of women in their administration of fairs and bazaars—an important branch of the public service that has fallen almost entirely into their hands. An endeavor is made to admit nothing impracticable for women living remote from the large centres, and at the same time to guide them in the use of the things which are about them. As the question of expense is always important, the prices of materials have been given ; but it must be understood that various causes make these variable, and that, though exact for the moment, they should be considered as approximate.

CONTENTS.

SKILFUL SUSY.

MATERIALS.

LINEN goods are among the most desirable of all materials used in embroidery, and no work is too elaborate to be lavished upon them.

BUTCHERS' LINEN is used for buffet covers, toilet sets, splashers, tea cloths. That used is the soft finish from 16 to 27 inches wide, varying in quality, and from 20 to 40 cents a yard.

BOLTING CLOTH is a transparent canvas, resembling pineapple silk, although the latter has much less firmness of texture. It is used for very delicate tidies and bureau covers, with silk embroidery and transparent washes.

CHINESE GRASS CLOTH is used for the same purposes, but is much cheaper. Price, from 35 cents to $2.50 a yard.

KENSINGTON CRAPE is a yellow-white material, about three quarters of a yard wide, suitable for bureau covers. Price, 35 cents.

MECCA CLOTH is a species of crape, with narrow cross stripes in color on white and light-colored grounds. It is from 1 to 2 yards wide. Price, $1 a yard.

MADRAS MUSLIN, used for draperies, is conspicuous for its soft folds, body, and for the soft color of its designs.

It is 50 inches wide, and ranges from 50 cents to $3.75 a yard.

Momie Cloth has a pebbled surface, and comes in white, cream, gray, light blue, and old gold tints. It is not as much used as plainer surfaces and lighter textures. It is 18 inches to a yard wide. Price, from 40 to 75 cents.

Bolton Sheeting has a diagonal twill, and is used for portières, table and bed spreads. It has an ivory tint that is very agreeable. It is 2 yards wide. Price, $1.25.

Batiste in white and cream tints makes desirable aprons, pin-cushion covers, and draperies. It is 46 inches wide. Price, 45 cents.

Linen Canvas comes in the same widths and for the same price as momie cloth, but is better adapted for the German cross stitch and for darned work than momie cloth.

Congress Canvas is a coarse, even-meshed grenadine a yard wide. It is an admirable ground for embroidery, especially for cross stitch in silks and crewels. Price, 58 cents a yard.

German Canvas resembles congress canvas, but has a firmer, closer mesh. It comes in white and cream tints, 18 inches wide. Price, 50 cents.

Eider Canvas is a pretty texture made by a group of threads in one mesh. It is 18 inches wide. Price, 40 cents.

Java Canvas consists of groups of threads in close meshes, with soft body. It comes in white, cream, gray, and other tints. It is especially suitable for cross and Holbein stitches.

Tapestry Canvas is a species of close, firm, repped canvas, on which tapestry and Gobelin colors are used. It comes from 36 to 122 inches wide. Price, $2.50 and $8 a yard.

FAYAL CRASH.—This is a very firm linen, gray in color, suitable for screens, or anything which requires a firm surface. It is especially good for painting in oils or water colors. Outline stitch can also be used on it. Width, 18 to 23 inches. Price, 25 to 30 cents.

SATEEN is found in all dark colors. It is not as much used as formerly. Width, 50 inches. Price, $2.50.

TURCOMAN has a beautiful silk pile resembling chenille. It is found in all colors. Width, 50 inches. Price for pile on one side, $2 up ; on both sides, $7.50. This in portières needs no lining.

JUTE VELOUR resembles Turcoman, but the pile is made of linen. The texture is consequently wirier, but the effect is very good. Used for hangings, sofa covers, and cushions. Price for single-faced, $2.50.

BRIDGEWATER CRICKETING FLANNEL.—A thick, soft flannel suitable for baby blankets. Designs most effective in chenille. Width, 27 inches. Price, $1.30.

ENGLISH EIDER-DOWN FLANNEL.—This comes in colors. It has a thick, soft, matted pile. It is also used for baby afghans. Price, $1.50.

LIBERTY SILKS.—These are thin India silks, which take their name from the English house that imports them. They come in what are known as art shades, and are used in tidies, cabinet and library curtains. Width, 36 inches. Price, $1.75.

CHINESE SILKS.—Silks greatly resembling those above for the same purposes and price.

AMERICAN ART SILKS equal these in tint and color, and are a trifle less in price. These also come in very attractive designs.

SILK TAPESTRY CANVAS.—These are 50 inches wide, and are used in portières, curtains, table covers, and screens. Price, $6 a yard.

BLUE DENIM.—In cheap materials nothing is more valuable for color. The coarse qualities that sell for 12 cents a yard are better in color than the finer, of which the blue is too intense.

JAPANESE CHINTZ.—This comes in all colors mixed with gold, and is useful in almost every way as a decorative material. Width, 36 inches. Price, 50 cents.

EMBROIDERY MATERIALS.

EMBROIDERY cottons come in all colors, of which most are fast; but the browns, reds, and blues are most satisfactory. The French and English cottons have the reputation of being more durable than the American. The French A B C cotton is a little smoother than the other cottons.

The best crewels also are the English and French. The former come in the best shades, according to our modern ideas. These are what are variously known as antique tints and art shades. Crewel by the dozen skeins costs 40 cents; by the single skein, 4 cents; 12 cents a hank.

FILO-FLOSS.—This is also called wash silk. It comes in skeins. Do not get that with black labels, for the colors are not warranted. Filo-floss, since it comes in strands, can be used for heavy embroidery, or, separated into threads, can be used in fine outlining. Price, 8 cents a skein; 85 cents by the dozen.

FILOSELLE.—This is used for filling, and, coming in strands, can also be separated into threads. It comes in two qualities—all silk and silk and linen. Filoselle, by couching either in single or double strands, makes a desirable cord-like outline when the single thread is used in the embroidery, thus getting variety of effects with the same material.

CHENILLE.—This is most suitable for plushes and flannel. Different makes have different sized skeins. Price, 40 cents a dozen.

ARRASENE.—This is the handsomest and most expensive of embroidery materials. It resembles chenille, but is flat and more suitable for leaves. Price, 35 cents a dozen skeins.

ETCHING SILK is a very fine silk used in outlining on doylies. Price, 6 cents a spool.

GOLD THREAD.—This is both coarse and fine. The best—the least likely to tarnish—is the Japanese gold thread. As gold thread is expensive, it is used generally as couching, in which case none is wasted on the wrong side. There are grades fine enough to be used in outlining, as silk is used. Price, 25 cents a hank ; 20 to 40 cents a spool.

TINSEL CORD BALLS.—These are found in all colors, and have an iridescent effect. They must always be couched down, as they are fragile and cannot be dragged through stuffs. Used in outlining, they are very effective. They can also be crocheted when no strain is required. Price, 15 cents a ball.

RIBBO-SENE.—This is a new material, crinkled in texture, and is used in ribbon work instead of narrow ribbons. Price, 5 cents a skein.

BRAIDENE is a new ribbon the width of daisy ribbon, but with a grain resembling Ottoman ribbon. This is used in ribbon work, and gives a feeling of texture ; for example, in rendering the large yellow Maximilian daisies or in snowballs the effect is better than when daisy ribbon is used.

METAL ORNAMENTS.—Hammered copper coins, gilt coins and sequins, stars, and crescents are used as finish for decorative articles instead of fringes. Price, 15 to 25 cents a dozen.

SPANGLES are used in embroidery with good effect, especially with tinsel cord and arrasene. Price, 10 to 15 cents a dozen.

PINE CONES AND BUTTON BALLS.—These are also used as finish for scarf, table covers, and other draperies, by covering them with bronze paint. They are suspended singly by a cord.

TASSELS.—These of every description can be bought in the form of silk pompons, plush cones, plush balls, plush crescents, at prices ranging from 90 cents to $2.50 a dozen. Beautiful tassels are made by combing out filoselle or crewel, and giving it a fine flossy effect. Short, bell-like tassels made of cream-colored filoselle, with gay silk threads of different colors outside, make most desirable tassels for light draperies.

EMBROIDERY STITCHES.

A FEW simple directions and illustrations may not be amiss concerning stitches used in embroidery and some definition of the terms used in this book.

STEM STITCH, South Kensington stitch, and feather stitch, as it is variously called, is familiar to almost every woman. As South Kensington and feather stitch, it is used in filling; as stem stitch and outline stitch, it is used in defining forms. In every way it is the most valuable and effective stitch used in embroidery.

BUTTON-HOLE STITCH, chain stitch, satin stitch, herring-

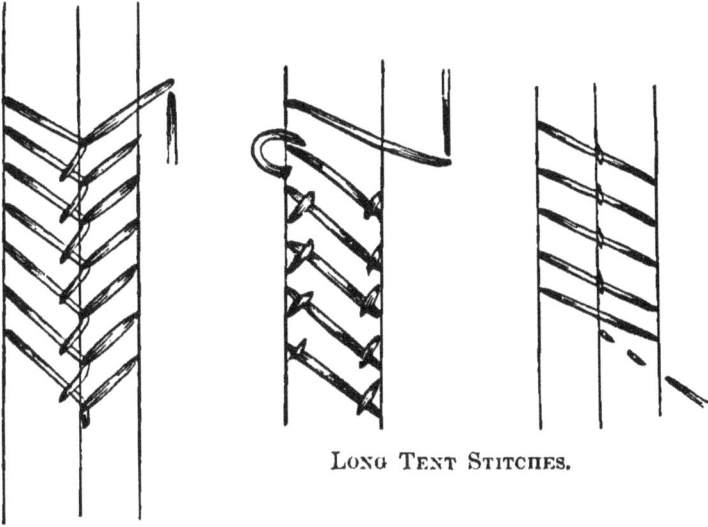

LONG TEXT STITCHES.

bone stitch, tent stitch, and plain cross stitch need no comment. There are, however, a variety of cross stitches very valuable.

PERSIAN CROSS STITCH has the cross at one end of the stitch instead of in the centre, and, in fact, is very much like the herring-bone stitch.

LONG TEXT STITCH is agreeably varied by crossing both ends and by catching down the middle by a straight stitch.

TURKISH CROSS STITCH consists of filling in the design by gradated cross

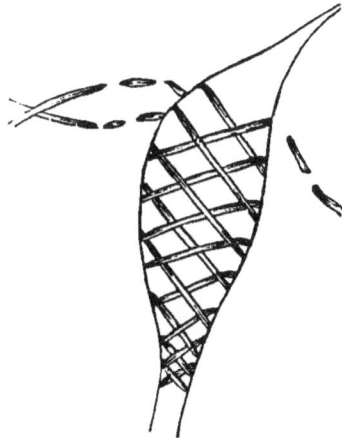

TURKISH CROSS STITCH.

stitches the length that the form demands rather than by a number of cross stitches.

HOLBEIN STITCH is used when the stitches can be counted. Java canvas is a suitable material. The stitch is, in fact, the seamstress' back stitch, but used with great regularity and in the production of many forms. Gilt braid inserted under a Greek fret made in Holbein stitch is very effective in making borders. It is useful to unite cross stitch with the Holbein stitch. The former is used in the ornament within borders of Holbein stitch.

PLATT STITCH is used also with Holbein and cross stitch in geometrical figures on any material in which the threads can be counted.

DARNED STITCH, next to outline stitch, is one of the most valuable used in embroidery. It is used in two ways. In pattern darning the ground is treated with darned stitch, which leaves the design in relief. When the darned stitch is used as part of the design it indicates

DARNED STITCHES.

the shading. Every housewife who uses prevention against the thin places in a stocking knows the stitch. In pattern drawing the ground is soon covered with regular stitches of filoselle. In indicating shading embroidery silk or cotton in single strands is more suitable.

In using darned stitch on the background attention must be paid to the tints used, since, as the ground shows through, a resultant tint from the union of the two colors in the eye is effected. In general the tint used should be somewhat darker than the ground. In using pongee, for example, one would take a yellowish brown filoselle. This, however, is not an absolute rule; for a different tint, but related in quality, as yellowish pink, warm pale blue, or olive green, could be judiciously used.

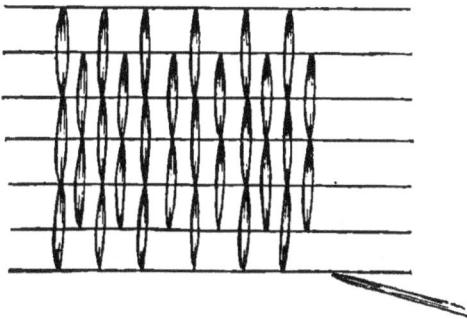

CUSHION BACKGROUND STITCH.

The design may be left without an outline, but it is perhaps more satisfactory to outline the forms in a still deeper tint. Other stitches, if desired, can be used in the design, but the simple, broad effect is more pleasing.

CUSHION BACKGROUND STITCH is, in fact, a species of darning, as the illustrations given indicate. This for the most part is used on canvas.

COUCHING is the term used when the embroidery material is not carried on to the under side of the fabric. The crewel, gilt thread, or whatever is used is laid on to the tracing, and is caught down by stitches of fine silk.

A great variety of effects is thus secured both in texture and color. Bold outlines are obtained by using several strands of crewel or double filoselle. Gilt thread and tinsel cord are always couched down. Solid designs are made in this way. Color effects are secured by couching in colors, the nearness of the stitch or remoteness giving gradations of color. The needle is brought up on side of the thread and is put through directly opposite on the other side.

DRAWN WORK.

This is the refinement of needlework, and can be made on fine materials as exquisite as lace. Learn on coarse linen. Pull the threads according to the width of the

No. 1.

insertion to be made, or if the design is to be in squares or groups of threads, draw the threads in that way. The simplest form of drawn work is to hem-stitch the threads into groups at each side. The next is to gather these groups by threes and fours into one thread at the centre, using chain stitch to hold them securely. From this point the design can be as elaborate as one chooses. The threads may be drawn to the depth of a quarter of a yard if desired. Illustration No. 2, for example, can be carried to any width. The second line in No. 2, it will be observed, is carried from one side of the centre line to the other, making a curve. Where several lines are made when they cross the centre line between the groups, it is well to make the centre solid by weaving over and under with a needle and thread, or by taking the lines in groups.

No. 2.

In designs like Nos. 1 and 3, which are most suitable for bureau covers, the edges of the squares should be

No. 3.

lightly whipped to keep the threads in place. The design No. 1 should be done in half-inch squares.

Drawn work should be done in frames. Linen thread
is best for this purpose. For coarse material use coarse
thread, and *vice versa*.

RIBBON WORK.

This is a revival of work carried to great perfection
by Marie Antoinette and the gay ladies of her court. It
consists in making dainty flowers and forms out of very
narrow ribbon, now known to the trade as Daisy ribbon.
This ribbon is drawn through the goods with a large
needle, or, if necessary, a hole is first punched. The
flower is then formed with the fingers. Forget-me-nots,

daisies, and such flowers are the most suitable. The outer edge of the petals are caught down with a stitch of silk. The foliage can be embroidered if preferred.

What is known as ribbon work, but improperly, brings pieces of silk into use. Wild roses, buttercups, dogwood, rosebuds, are formed by pieces of silk laid on, pinched into shape with the fingers, and neatly fastened down. Very good effects in drawing are gotten in this way.

Fine imitations of snowballs are given by filling convex in shape, and then tacking on to it numbers of small bits of white daisy silk cut into pieces three quarters of an inch long, diagonal at the edges, crossing them, and catching them down in the centre with a stitch of yellow silk. Pile these one on another. The effect is very good.

DESIGNS.

BEAUTY of design is by no means proportioned to the amount of labor involved. Some of the most effective designs and methods employed are the simplest. Other things being equal, conventional designs are better and easier than realistic designs. The latter, to be good, should be perfect in drawing and color, and this requires a knowledge of nature that few have.

We owe to the Japanese much of our lately acquired skill in the choice of design, and also how much may be effected in slight ways. A few instances of these will not be amiss.

DISKS are circles used singly and in groups, balancing one another in a certain area. They are filled in with some design. Crescents and other simple forms are used in the same manner. Single flowers, such as the pansy, pelargonium, or daisy, are so distributed.

CRACKLE or ZIGZAGS are used in breaking up the ground, and generally serve also to connect some set forms, such as the disks and their substitutes.

WATER LINES indicate, as their name implies, the existence of water, and is used to break up the ground in

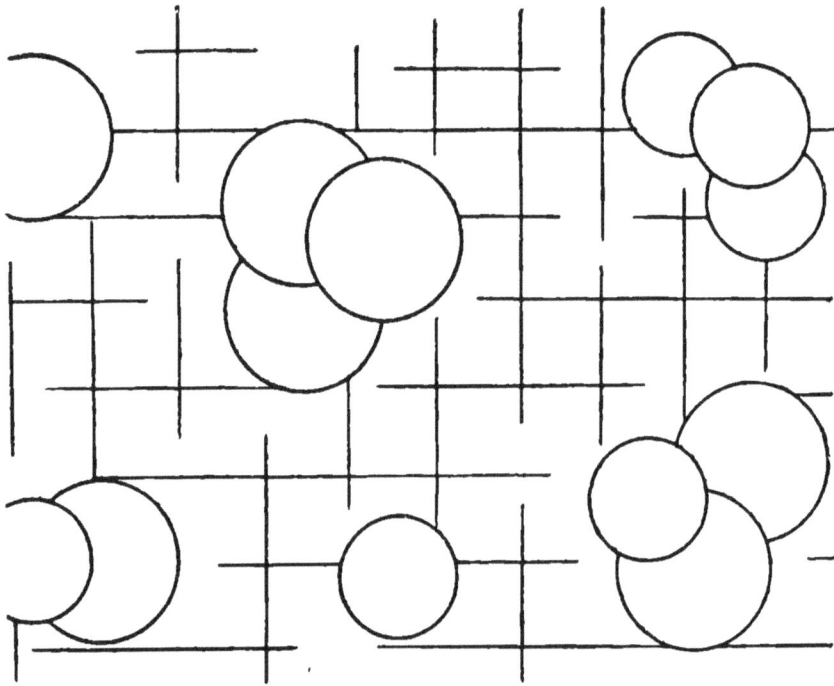

connection with aquatic plants and animals. This is not obligatory, and they can be used amid other surroundings.

CLOUD FORMS.—These are a Japanese fashion of representing aerial effects, and serve to break up the surface in the way described above.

FLIGHTS OF BIRDS.—These are another instance of forms barely indicated serving a decorative purpose.

FRET AND DOUBLE FRET.—It is difficult to trace this form to any nation, but it is a most valuable aid in decoration.

SPIDER'S WEB.—In more realistic forms this is one of the most valuable. It will also serve to connect set forms, as do crackle lines.

RENAISSANCE SCROLLS.—These scroll forms with floriations are among the richest decorative forms. They are beautifully filled in with couchings of gold thread with colored silks, using the deeper tints at the base and growing lighter toward the edges. They can also be done in Kensington stitch and in outline stitch.

ARABESQUES.—These are Moorish forms used in borders, and can be executed very much in the same manner as the scrolls spoken of above.

Mosaics.—These are geometrical forms chiefly taken from the Moorish decoration. They are very effective in appliqué. Making, we will say, the ground in colored silks or brocades, cut out the intersecting forms of plush, and couch them down with crewels.

COLOR.

There are two ways of using color—in harmonies and by contrasts. Harmonies in color are secured by using tints that lead into one another, or with some common bond of relationship. For example, you have a piece of red plush to embroider. In the groundwork of your design use a deeper shade of red, and gradually lighten the tints until in the high lights the color is carried up to light pinks. If the material is warm in color the reds must be kept warm ; if cold, the reds must be kept cold.

To illustrate a more elaborate harmony of color : we have, let us say, a bouquet of roses. The color begins at the base in deep red roses, with foliage of dark greens. In both the reds and greens there is a filling of yellow—that is to say, the colors are warm. Working up from the base we add more yellow to the reds and more yellow to the greens, each becoming lighter, until, when we have reached the top, we may have roses and buds of pure warm yellow and tender, yellowish-green foliage.

To do this requires a certain feeling for color, lest the lack of it admits some tint not of the same quality. A purplish red or a blue green would make a discord just as would a false note in music.

Contrasts in color consist of putting colors in juxtaposition, such as red, green, blue, yellow, purple—colors not immediately related. In using colors by contrast it is of paramount importance that, no matter how different the colors, the same quality of color must be preserved. The great division of tints into cold and warm must be regarded. If any one will study for a short time those modern colors known to us as antique tints, or the frank use of color made by the Japanese, they will get an appreciation of this distinction. The Japanese bring the most diverse colors together with unerring instinct by simply observing this one fact. To illustrate its necessity, place a bit of old-fashioned cherry on a piece of stuff in which are warm reds and greens. The discord is at once felt. Colors are warm through yellow and cold through blue. This is a distinction sufficiently broad for ordinary use.

Something has been said of resultant tints. These are the union of different colors in the eye, producing an entirely different tint. Thus, a small design in positive blue stencilled on a bright brick-dust hue produces a purple in the eye. The use of tints this way by couching gilt thread with colored silks—red, blue, purple—produces a beautiful flush of color like none of the tints used. Shading in flowers by irregular stitches of different colors showing the ground beneath is effected in this way. If one studies the petals of a natural flower it will be observed that the lines of shading vary in tint. No better guide can be recommended.

PAINTS, AND HOW TO USE THEM.

Oil paints to be used on stuffs should be first placed on coarse brown paper, that it may absorb the superfluous oil, and thus avoid running. In using oil paints on plush it is necessary to have a stiff brush. In painting a large leaf the palette-knife, for laying on the paint, may be used to advantage.

Use water color in thin washes. Sizing and other media destroy the transparency. If necessary, put a little gum-arabic in the water. Use water with care. It is a good plan after dipping the brush in water to draw it across a piece of soap before putting it in the paint. This keeps the water from running. Take up no more paint than is necessary on the brush.

Always draw with the brush if possible. It saves time, and gives a certain freedom to the design. This demands, however, a certain facility ; and if the hand is not sure use tracing-paper. In using light colors on dark grounds it is necessary to use Chinese white underneath the color.

Aniline dyes are used for transparent washes on thin curtains, draperies, tidies, and linen goods. These are desirable, as the tint becomes part of the fabric and will not fade. Buy the dry aniline dyes that are soluble in alcohol, using just enough of the spirit to take up the dye. Bottle the solution. In using it dilute or reduce to the tint desired. The dyes that are only soluble in alcohol are brighter and more durable than those that will dissolve in water.

Lustra paints are bronze powders of various hues, which give prismatic effects when applied. They are sold at prices varying from 15 to 25 cents a bottle or package, and with a medium, costing 15 cents a bottle. With this medium the powder is mixed to the consistency of cream, and should be applied with a good stiff brush. When used on smooth surfaces the paint should be thinned ; on rough surfaces, such as velveteen or plush, mix it stiffer, and take care in applying it that it shall not appear streaky.

FLITTER AND BROCADE are iridescent powder paints. The design is first covered with a thin white varnish; on this the powder is sprinkled. The effect is much more glistening and brilliant than lustra painting, and is equally permanent. They can be used on any surface, such as baskets, bottles, palm-leaf fans, crocheted work, pine cones, or other rustic ornaments.

GOBELIN TAPESTRY PAINTS.—These are bought in liquid form. They cannot be diluted. The lightest shades are reached by using them very thin. Deeper tints are secured by repeating the color.

SUGGESTIONS.

Do not have embroidery frames too large to handle conveniently. If the material is larger than the frame, and will crease by rolling, baste a piece of cotton on the under side of the material, and fasten the cotton to the frame. This will admit of stretching without injuring the stuff.

If the embroidery cannot be pressed out without injury and is a little pulled, dampen the wrong side with the following mixture: Gum arabic, one ounce; water, three ounces; one teaspoonful of sugar; two teaspoonfuls of alcohol. Let it dry in the frame.

The same mixture can be used with water colors on fabrics where there is danger of their running.

In embroidering or painting mottoes or texts as a part of decoration, group the letters or words irregularly. Make the first letter of the prominent words in large capitals.

Etching on linen, as it is called, is done with a fine brush and India ink.

At almost all stores where artists' materials can be had, small ornaments in holly-wood, such as fans, crescents, paddles, oars, boxes, plaques, lawn-tennis bats, palettes, racks, rolling-pins, irons, rudders, easels, wood bellows, sickles, needle-book covers, anchors, can be bought.

Patterns for doylies, tidies, bureau covers, and for flannel skirts can be bought, and the designs transferred to the material by pressing with a warm iron.

The old-fashioned method of pouncing to transfer designs is still practised. Trace the pattern with pin-holes, and if desired to preserve it, prick it on to flannel with a needle fastened into a piece of cork. Make a pad of pieces of flannel cloth folded firmly. Dip this into powdered charcoal and go over the pattern on the stuff, blowing off the superfluous powder. Trace the pattern after with a fine brush or pencil.

Embroidery on wash goods is effective when the outline is done in color with an inner line of white, and the veining also done in white.

Patterns for bears, elephants, rabbits, camels, mice, horses, pigs, etc., to be made of Canton flannel for children, can be bought at pattern stores, with instructions for their use.

Such forms as maple leaves may be better outlined by using long and short stitch perpendicularly instead of the usual outline stitch.

Lace may be made more ornamental by painting the pattern in water color, or by the use of bronze paints. In this way it can be toned into the color of the material it trims.

Designs cut out of cretonne and over-worked with silk and tinsel cord are used on the most expensive materials.

The cut forms for paper flowers, with directions how

to make them, can be bought. Use paste, not mucilage, in sticking tissue paper.

Plush flowers that are bought can be used for set figures connected by crackle lines with good effect.

Tendrils are made by using two rows of filoselle and couching it down.

Buy shoemakers' paste to use in pasting embroidery when it is to be appliquéd on the ground.

Endeavor always to utilize materials at hand. They often suggest new ways of doing things that prove very desirable.

Learn to find designs in head-pieces and tail-pieces in books and magazines, on pieces of stuffs, books, covers.

Never attempt to put on paint in decoration evenly. Charm lies in variety of tint. In using metallic tints this should be especially observed.

HOUSEHOLD DRAPERIES.

Portières.—It is impossible to describe the numerous ways in which these are made. For summer, Madras muslin and India cottons are very suitable and no trouble. A suitable decoration for the upper part of a portière is a network of fringe, with long, irregular tassels ; these are made of skeins of crewel or of silk. Never put tassels or fringe on the bottom of a portière ; but on the handsomest portières a network of these are put on the curtain high enough not to hang below the edge. Twisted and braided strands of crewel and silk with loose ends and of irregular lengths are used often instead of fringe.

Very simple decoration is all that is required on portières, as the folds obscure the design. Disks and crescents outlined and darned inside are very good ; also large flowers washed in disks or embroidered by simply indicating the lines of shading.

RAG SILK PORTIÈRES may be made attractive by arranging the colors properly. Mass a great deal of gray silk together for bars, and fill in with masses of bright colors. Yellows are very good. Dye old white ribbons yellow and red with the prepared dyes.

PORTIÈRES OF TAPESTRY CANVAS, with appliqué of plush circles connected by plush bars, fastened with couchings of double filoselle, are extremely handsome and easily made.

BATISTE CURTAIN.—Draw the design either as a border or as cross bands. A large, flowing, continuous pattern is advisable, or oblong sections containing geometrical lines. Wash in the colors with aniline dyes. Outline the forms with silk of the same color, but a darker shade than is used in the wash. Simply hem the curtain, and finish with bell tassels.

INDIA SILK CURTAIN.—A curtain of a pale terra-cotta tint has the design in an open-petalled flower and foliage. The color is washed in in deeper tones, and the outline is in tinsel cord. This should be done in a frame.

VESTIBULE CURTAIN.—Écru Chinese silk. Draw geometrical designs, concentric circles, and such forms, and outline in dark red silk.

BOOK-CASE CURTAINS.—Make the curtains of yellow silk, and simply hem and finish with little bell tassels of combed-out filoselle mixed with gilt.

CABINET CURTAINS.—Make these daintily of pale Nile green, shrimp pink, turquoise blue, or some thin silk that will be in harmony with the surroundings. Cover these with lines of gilt crackle.

BED SPREADS.—Take a piece of Bolton sheeting the required length. Have it stamped with a large "all-over" pattern of conventionalized peonies. Outline the flowers in an open button-hole three quarters of an inch deep; the button-hole shows the goods between the stitches. Use crewel of dull light red. Vein the flowers and leaves in outline stitch. Use heavy strands of the crewel in couchings to indicate the other bold forms. It is much more work, but the effect is very fine to darn the ground in several strands of the crewel. Make a border all around with lines of outline stitch in groups. Edge with deep Smyrna lace.

LINEN BED SPREAD.—Make a border by drawing threads, and an edge by fringing out the linen. Across the lower end of the spread draw a design of locust branch, with leaves, flowers, and twigs. Do the twigs in brown silks, solid in Kensington stitch. The leaves are also solid Kensington stitch in greens. The flowers are in shaded pinks. In the upper part of the spread indicate the ends of branches, and embroider in the same way. In the spaces draw broken bits of sprays and flowers, and here and there a single leaf or flower. The border is filled up with these bits. This is ambitious work, but may suggest other work in kind not so diffi-cult. In doing these large pieces it is better to get out long disused quilting frames. The work can be kept much smoother and neater in frames. As a suggestion, use disks in the ornament inclosing flowers—clover blos-soms, for example. Make Japanese water marks or sky marks in the spaces.

LAMBREQUINS.—Plush, velvet, and velveteen are the suitable materials for mantel lambrequins. Felt is no longer used, being ugly in texture and attracting moths. Draped lambrequins are the prettiest. Often these are of stuff alone, without any finish or ornament, the beauty lying in the folds, which are easily kept in place. Every mantel should have a board to rest on top, on which the lambrequin is draped.

PLUSH LAMBREQUIN.—Take two pieces of dark blue plush, each half the length of the mantel. On each of these arrange sprigs of flowers cut out of lace patterns, and embroider them on with colored silks and spangles. The eye, assisted by the markings of the pattern, will need no further guide. Hem up or line with light blue marcelline silk. Finish with bell tassels of silk. Fasten the two pieces up, making them meet in the centre, where a large bow of wide blue satin or brocaded ribbon is placed. Gather back each piece curtain-wise about half way down, and fasten. Let the ends hang straight.

PORTABLE LAMBREQUIN.—Lay on a mantel-board a piece of gray plush. Drape, leaving deep scollop in the centre. Where this ends fasten yellow Chinese silk and gather it back curtain-wise; tie with yellow ribbons, and stick in peacock feathers.

BRACKET LAMBREQUIN.—Take Madras muslin a quarter of a yard deep. Outline the designs with silver tinsel cord, and vein with silks, covering the design thinly. Finish with a fringe, with tinsel in the fringe.

TABLE COVER of crimson tapestry canvas. Make the border of two rows of circles and bars placed four inches apart in length, and two inches apart in height. These are an appliqué of crimson plush couched down with deep red filoselle doubled. Tassels at each corner.

HOLBEIN TABLE COVER.—This is a gray linen fringed and knotted at the edges. The design is copied in Holbein and cross stitch in red from the famous table-cover in the picture of the Madonna by Holbein in the Dresden Gallery.

SMALL TABLE COVERS are made of thin silks in art shades, lined and faced up with brocaded silks or handsome Japanese chintzes.

TIDIES.—Never make a tidy that cannot be washed or cleaned. Those of thin materials, such as bolting cloth or grass linen, are the handsomest. Edge them with fine Smyrna lace. Line with silk.

BOLTING CLOTH TIDY.—Take a piece of bolting cloth twelve by sixteen inches. Hem with one row of hemstitching. Outline a group of disks in reddish brown. Wash in the disks a pale red, and paint in each a wild rose in deeper tints. In some disks show the flower in perspective; in others only part of the flower. Connect the various disks by irregular lines. This method of treating bolting cloth tidies may be varied in tints and design.

CHINESE GRASS LINEN TIDY.—Take an oblong piece of grass cloth twenty-four by fourteen inches. Define a border by two rows of outline stitching four inches apart. In the border arrange small disks in the manner illustrated. Outline these disks with outline stitch. Fill them with darned stitch of yellowish-pink filoselle. Use a deeper tint in the outline. Below this border make a border of drawn work, and finish with lace.

IVY LEAF TIDY.—Make a tidy similar to that above, and use ivy leaf forms just as disks are used. They should be veined instead of darned. Clover leaves can be used in the same way, and sweet-brier will also serve.

GRASS LINEN SQUARE TIDY.—Take a square piece of grass linen, hem and hem-stitch it all around. Embroider in the centre a group of roses as if lying in a heap. Use silk and satin stitch. Reds and yellows are the best combinations.

GERMAN CANVAS TIDY.— Scarf tidy twenty-seven

inches long. Draw out at each end groups of threads wide enough to admit the narrowest ribbon. Leave a space just a little less wide. Make a stripe in this way, and weave colored ribbons in and out. A border of drawn work on each side is an addition. Fringe out the stuff a finger's length deep at the ends.

HOLBEIN TIDY.—An oblong tidy made of German canvas twenty-seven inches long. Each end is embroidered almost a quarter of a yard deep with a conventional border of red and blue in Holbein and cross stitch. Fringe out the ends.

SCARF TIDY.—Take a strip of India silk or the American silk of the same texture a yard and a half long. What are known as art shades are more attractive. Such are yellow-pinks, green-blues. Define a border by four rows of outline stitch, or by couching tinsel cord. The design inside is groups of dogwood blossoms arranged just as disks are used. If the border is couched in tinsel cord the flowers are treated in the same way. If the border is outlined, we will say, in red, the silk being yellow pink, the flowers should be also outlined. Put the centres in knot stitch. The ends are hemmed, and edged with fluffy tassels made by combing out filoselle and covering with gay threads. When finished the centre is gathered up in two loops and tied with a satin ribbon matching the tint.

PONGEE TIDY.—Take a strip of pongee a yard and a half long ; fringe out the ends : make a heading by knotting. Embroider in silks a stiff little row of violets, buttercups, and primroses, with foliage. Tie into a scarf tidy.

PONGEE TIDY.—Oblong tidy with a border, in which are daisies made by couching double white filoselle, with centres of knot stitch in yellow filoselle. Begin by taking the white filoselle from the centre and catching it down at the circumference. The daisy can be drawn in every way in this manner.

TRANSPARENT TIDY.—An oblong piece of bolting cloth hemmed with hem-stitch. Wash in pale browns and yellows a design of horse-chestnut leaves and burs. Outline with brown silk. This is exquisite in design and color.

CHAIR BACK.—Take two pieces of gay sprigged cretonne. Measure them by the size of a plain wooden chair. Put them together and bind the edges with ribbons. Put bows at the two upper corners. These chair backs are intended to slip over one's chair in a public dining-room during the summer to protect the backs of delicate dresses from the chair backs, that are apt to be soiled by the waiters' fingers.

More ornamental chair backs are made of Swiss, sprigged or plain, and have the initials embroidered in outline stitch. Two constitute a set, since they occasionally require washing.

SPLASHERS.—Aquatic designs very appropriately are used on splashers. Water-lilies, storks among flags, done in outline stitch on momie cloth, are very useful. Designs can be bought of boats, with children and boating parties of grown people. Children on the beach, with water-lines indicating the sea, are also used. Broken water-lines, with set shells and sea-weed interspersed, are suitable. A border with these for the centre put around a splasher is good. Conventional designs appeal to the eye longer than the outline sketches. A splasher put beneath a looking-glass can have embroidered on it Burns's lines :

> " O wad some power the giftie gie us
> To see oursel's as ithers see us."

THE DINING-ROOM.

BUFFET COVERS.—These are necessary on every buffet
or sideboard with a marble top against possible break-
age ; otherwise they are suitable and befitting a dining-
room. Undoubtedly the revival of antique furniture has
brought into vogue old customs. Linen is always used.
Butchers' linen is most commonly employed, the grain
being prominent. Fine linen can be wrought into covers like lace work. The ends are fringed and knotted as
a finish. Outline stitch in white, red, and blue is generally used in the decoration. The fringe and ornament
are at the ends. Usually a suitable motto is carried across.

CRESCENT BUFFET COVER.—Long strip of butchers'
linen fringed at the ends. Scattered over it are crescents
in groups of one, twos, and threes arranged like disks.
These are in outline stitch in blue and darned centres.

DRAWN BUFFET COVER.—Take a strip of fine linen ;
fringe the edges ; make a band of insertion of drawn
work, like design No. 3, not less than one eighth of a
yard wide. It may be fully a quarter of a yard. The
ornament must hang over the sides.

DUTCH BUFFET COVER.—The name comes from the
design copied from old Dutch cloths. These are usually
maids serving, men and women drinking, in connection
with much florid ornament. The outlines are double in
two colors. The leaves and flowers are filled with work.
Often there are cross diagonal lines of white caught down
at the intersections with a stitch of color. The draperies
of the figures are all indicated in lines of color. Dutch
texts are introduced in the ornament.

TEA CLOTHS AND TRAY CLOTHS.—The fashion of after-
noon teas and little tables demand tea cloths and tray

cloths. These are usually square, and are fringed all around. They may be simply hemmed with a line of hem-stitching. A band of drawn work, as designs Nos. 1 and 2, are as handsome and dainty as one can desire. In designs outline stitch with fine etching silk or filo-floss and cottons warranted to wash should be used.

SCARF TEA CLOTH.—This is oblong; the ends are fringed as in a buffet cover. A design in Dutch work across the edge is very suitable. A conventional pattern, as Greek fret, may be introduced all around, or arrange disks all over the cloth, in which are small ewers or champagne glasses or cups and saucers in outline sketch.

SQUARE TEA CLOTH.—This is ornamented at the corner with four little girls seated eating from out a bowl in outline stitch in red.

JACK HORNER TEA CLOTH.—This design and that above are suitable for children's table. The design relates the history of Jack Horner in the corners. First, he sits in the corner with his pie. He puts in his thumb. He pulls out a plum. Then he is filled with admiration of himself.

DESIGNS FOR CORNERS.—These can be bought. Most suitable are sets of tea things; ewers and glasses; dishes filled with oysters, fruit; salad bowl and spoon; celery glass with celery; game hanging from knots of ribbon. Conventional designs are palm leaves, crackle lines, broken straight and horizontal lines connecting set figures. A list of suitable mottoes is given in another place. The work should all be daintily done.

DOYLIES.—These should not be over six inches square, since their only use is to protect the fruit-plate from being scratched by the finger-bowl. They should be of the sheerest finest linen bolting cloth or pineapple silk, and

the edges always fringed three quarters of an inch deep.
Make them in sets of six or a dozen. Choose a coherent
series of designs, but make each doyly different. Pineapple silk doyly can be ornamented in water colors or
dyes. Use silk or cotton on linen that will not fade in
washing. Etching silk, as it is called, for this purpose,
is spoken of in the chapter on embroidery materials. It
is used in outlining, and has the effect of a pen-and-ink
drawing, the sketch is so fine.

DESIGNS FOR DOYLIES.—Make a set in outline stitch, in
which fans of all kinds shall be sprinkled over the surface. Jugs, teapots, vases, flower-pots in antique blues,
pinks, greens, and reds will make another series. Different flowers, with bits of foliage, single petals strewn
apparently at haphazard over the texture, sea-weeds,
and shells form another series for doylies. Kate Greenaway figures, now so accessible in cuts of every description, will complete another series. Designs of fruits,
decanters, and glasses are admirable.

DRAWN WORK DOYLIES.—Nothing is more exquisite
than these. The chapter on drawn work gives suitable instructions. Simple doylies are made by a band of threads
three quarters of an inch drawn, and the edges button-
holed to keep the threads in place. Inside work a row of
forget-me-nots in blue silk.

TEA COSIES.—The Japanese send us tea cosies that
can be easily made by taking a piece of cotton batting,
glazed side out. Lay on it a piece of thin silk as a lining.
Mould or press this into a shape which will cover over the
tea-pot. It will be about eighteen inches wide and twelve
high for an ordinary sized tea-pot. Bind the lower
open edges with some pretty substantial stuff. Japanese
chintz with gold is what our neighbors use. The glazed
cotton part is painted lightly in water colors.

ENGLISH TEA COSIES.—These are a part of the furniture of every English table. They are the shape as described above. The outsides may be either of quilted silk or embroidered, as the fancy may dictate.

EGG COSIES.—These are suitable presents for bachelors. Take three pieces of white or colored satin four and a half inches wide, six inches high ; taper to a point ; embroider or paint each piece. A young fluffy chicken outlined by short, irregular strokes, either with paint or the needle, is a good design for one piece ; on another paint an empty shell ; on the third ornamental letters or initials. Line these pieces with a thin layer of cotton ; sew together, and cover the seams with gold cord. Line with thin silk. The shape is something that of a bishop's hat, but three-sided. Surmount with a little gold tassel.

SCREENS.

SCREENS.—Any carpenter can make the frame. If it is to be covered it will not require any finish. If not covered, have it of oak, cherry, ash, or walnut. Pine frames are good treated with ebony or cherry frames. It is a pretty fashion to have the upper part of the frame divided by a bar, and diamond or square lattice work inserted. The panels may be covered with fayal crash, cartridge paper, matting, split bamboo, rough canvas, gunny bags, old coffee sacking, or, in fact, with whatever is most convenient. Stretch the stuff smoothly, and tack on the edges furniture gimp.

CARTRIDGE PAPER SCREEN.—Two-leaved screen, each leaf covered on each side with gray cartridge paper. Paint in oils on athwart the leaf a branch of wisteria, large broad leaves and large clusters of flowers. On the reverse side, a tall towering stalk of cactus with deep red flowers. On the opposite side paint branches of pine and pine cones. On the reverse side of this leaf put the trumpet creeper, foliage and flowers. The painting should be done in broad, easy style.

MATTING SCREEN.—Very broad two-leaved screen for concealing entrance to kitchen in country house. Cover the panels with fine matting, such as cost fifty or sixty cents a yard. Paint across both leaves horizontal branches of grape-vine and fruit.

BAGGING SCREEN.—Cover with coarse bagging. Gild the panels, and overlay here and there with very thin reds and blue glazes, which give a sort of iridescence to the texture. Outline here disks singly and in groups in brown red. Paint in these in some design, such as a large flower or geometrical figures. On the ground put Japanese water marks—that is to say, broken lines in brown red and deep blue. If more work is wanted, large branches of fruit, oranges, apples, peaches, and plums are very effective.

FAYAL CRASH SCREENS.—Cover the panels with this material after it has been embroidered in outline stitch. A three-leaved fayal crash screen, with conventional designs of Juno, Venus, and Minerva in bold red outline stitch, is very nice. This is a low screen, not over two feet and a half high.

BURLAP SCREENS.—Cover the frame with burlap nailed tightly on. Outline some large flower and leaves all over the screen in gold. Put this in in each leaf in color. For example, on one leaf the flower will be in dull reds on a blue ground; on another, dull blue on red ground. These tints always change in intensity. Let it be a cardinal rule never to attempt to preserve a uniform tint.

Mix gold also with the tints. It is a good idea to underlie all the color with gold, and then allow it to shine through.

GUNNY BAG SCREENS.—Cover the screen with gunny bagging. Use the screen as a receptacle for palette scrapings. It is wonderful what fine effects can be had in this way—shining masses of color. It will, of course, take some time to finish. Such a screen should be in every studio.

BURLAP SCREENS.—Cover a frame with ordinary burlap. The color of this is very good, but it is usually treated in some way. A good way is to cut out the figures in cretonne. These are now so large that they are well adapted for this purpose. Japanese and Chinese designs, with figures, temples, and trees, with screaming, bright-hued birds, are often large enough to cover a screen. These are pasted on, and the edges button-holed loosely with crewel.

WATTEAU SCREENS have a plain wooden frame painted with enamel white paint. Touch it up with gold. Buy French cretonne in Watteau designs, shepherdesses, and fine ladies in landscape. Such a combination makes an attractive drawing-room screen, now that Louis XVI. styles are in vogue.

NURSERY SCREEN.—Cover with burlap, and paste on every sort of picture, Christmas or Easter card.

WOOD WORK.

DRESSING TABLE.—Have a carpenter make an oblong or semicircular frame for the table, with a straight board going up the back on which to attach the mirror. Cover the table back and flounce to the floor with pink or blue cambric. Make a puff or cover the mirror frame with the cambric. Use for outside covers dotted muslin edged with lace, and from the top over the mirror drape one long piece of muslin as curtains. This will serve as a model. India silk and flowered chintz can be also used. These prettily made would prove very saleable.

BABY'S RATTLE.—Have turned a smooth round stick a foot long and as thick as your finger. Wind this with ribbons. On the head fasten a bow of the same colors, and at the bottom tack four narrow ribbons so that there will be eight ends of different lengths. On the end of each ribbon attach a little brass ball or bell. This makes also a pretty favor for the German.

WOODEN TWO-SHOES are used for match safes. They are made ornamental by gilding, with bows painted on, and are hung by ribbons.

WOODEN EGGS, with holes bored in, are also used for match safes. The ornament consists of two chickens sketched on in light touches. Being exactly alike, they are "matches." The egg is suspended by ribbons nailed on at each side and tied in a bow.

BRASS LADDERS are used to mount thermometers. A support comes with the ladder such as accompany easels and photograph frames, but also of brass.

KEY AND SCISSORS RACK.—Take an oblong panel of wood eight inches long and five inches wide. Bevel the edges, or define with a gilt line. Screw in a row of little brass hooks. Below paint some design in water colors. The most popular ornament is the following verse in fancy letters :

> " Hang on this rack whatever you please—
> Button-hooks, scissors, and all of your keys.
> To keep you from losing, here is my art,
> You never can lose the key to my heart."

Hang it by rings or suspend by a ribbon. The rack may be covered with plush or brocaded goods instead of being decorated. Wooden padlocks are used as key racks. Sometimes they are covered with delicate plushes, the key-hole represented in gilt paint. A bow of ribbon is tied on the handle. Other forms are painted, black and white being used on the wood. A favorite device is an owl on a branch, with a crescent moon. Underneath are the lines :

> " Bird of wisdom, pray guard mo
> Against the loss of time or key ;"

or,

> " Shun the fate of Mother Hubbard,
> Nor lose the key that locks the cupboard ;"

or,

> " Lose the key, and very soon
> You're out of time and out of tune."

Small rolling-pins are made for dainty key racks. Several bars of music are drawn in on black on a gilt ground. Below is printed :

> " Until the proper key is found,
> Music is but discordant sound."

MILKING STOOLS.—Have a carpenter make old-fashioned milking stools, in which the three legs meet in the centre. Paint them a solid color, gild or bronze. Paint in the centre bouquets of daisies, roses, chrysanthemums, or geometrical designs, as in dull reds and blues on gold.

CHOPPING-BOWL PLAQUE.—Gild the inside, using a good deal of red in the gilt, and allow it to lighten toward the outer edge. Draw overlapping disks here and there with brown umber. In these disks outline great flowers, almost filling the disks. Allow large leaves in outline and filled in with greenish gilt to spring up, as it were, from one part of the edge around the disk. Opposite to this make a group of lines at right angles and about a part of a disk at the edge.

CIGAR BOXES.—Boxes of satin-wood and other fancy woods wide enough to lay the cigars in crosswise are decorated in water colors. Choose some pretty scroll design, and paint in reds and browns. This should be arranged as a border on top, and run around the sides. Enclosed in the border paint a monogram, initials, or the word cigars. The effect of the whole decoration is that of illumination.

CIGARETTE BOXES.—These are made like the above, the size being adapted to cigarettes, and the design proportioned accordingly. Conventional ornament is much more appropriate than flowers.

CARD COUNTERS.—These in white wood can be bought. The form is that of two palm leaves at different angles, with a crescent joining them. On one side paint around the palm small points of different colors. Between each point put a number up to ten in gilt, surrounded by a black circle. Draw fan lines in color down to the stick. Around the other palm paint the spot cards at different angles, and between each the numbers again. Draw the same fan lines again. On each palm is a small sword on a pivot as counter which must be silvered. Tie a small bow of ribbon on to the crescent. The same motto given for card boxes is here most appropriately introduced. The white holly form of the card counter can be bought at shops where such articles in wood for decorative purposes are sold.

CLOTHES-PIN NAPKIN HOLDER.—Gild old-fashioned clothes pins. Ornament with geometrical lines in blue and Indian red. Hold the napkin flat and slip in.

Thermometer Iron.—This is made of wood in the shape of an ordinary flat-iron, and painted black or given a coat of copper bronze. Another flat piece of wood the shape of the bottom is covered with crimson plush, and embroidered or painted. This is done toward one side ; on the other a flat thermometer is screwed. This piece is then fastened on to the bottom of the iron, which sits on ends.

Thermometer Panel.—A thin panel of white wood, with bevelled edge and a support for the back. The thermometer is fastened on to one side. The other is decorated with some flower and foliage. Beneath is painted in ornamental letters :

> " A silver ball in a crystal tube,
>   And it gently ebbs and flows
> To mark the strength of the north wind's blast,
>   Or time the bloom of the rose.''

FANCY CHAIRS.

Splint Sewing Chairs.—Take a plain, straight-back, low, splint-bottom rocking-chair. Make cushions for the back and seat of gray linen. But first on the back and seat draw designs of the pumpkin vine and flower. Outline these with brown. Wash in the leaves in thin transparent green and the flowers in yellow. Use of both colors a variety of tints. On the leaves, for example, there may be splotches of light yellow-green, as are seen in leaves lying in sunlight. Tie on with bows of yellow and green satin ribbon.

Or, instead of gray linen, take yellowish green velveteen. Line it with ticking and fasten it down tightly for the seat. But first ornament both seat and back with circles divided into geometrical forms, and paint these in in dull reds and blues. Moorish forms will give good ideas for such decoration. Make eyelets in the backs, and lace the back tightly on around the frame with silk cord of the tint of the ground. Brown velveteen or dark green and blue velveteen are good colors for such work.

CHILD'S ROCKING-CHAIR.—Take a strip of tapestry canvas and paint on it a spider's web and some vines. Make this into a cushioned back for a plain little wooden rocking-chair. Make a cushion to match. These may be made even handsomer by using richer materials.

Plain, rough, little wood rocking-chairs are painted black and varnished, or any solid tint, and ornamented with flowers on the back and seat. Paint also the word " Baby" in ornamental letters in gilt. Very pretty chairs are also made by stencilling simple patterns on the back in colors.

OLD CHAIRS.—These can be made very attractive by repainting in solid color, stencilling on designs on the back, and covering the seat with cushions of blue or crimson velours.

STEAMER CHAIRS.—Take off one arm, that they may be sat in with less trouble. Paint them with enamel black paint. Make cushions of gay cretonne or more handsome material, and swing a head cushion by a ribbon around the top.

FRAMING PICTURES.

THERE is no present more acceptable and no article more saleable than a picture. Photography reproduces works of art so perfectly that a good photograph is much

more desirable than an ordinary engraving. Pictures
should be framed with reference to their subject. This
gives the ingenuity great scope. A few examples will
suffice.

The picture is a photograph of a harvest scene. The
frame is of rough wood, which the tools have given additional roughness. In one corner is a small sickle.
The blade is made by taking out the wood in the required shape. This can easily be done with a hot poker,
the form having been previously drawn. The blade is
also sunk, but the roundness of the handle is indicated
by slight curves.

A marine is framed in rough boards ; over this a white
net is drawn tight. Through rings in the corners a rope
is passed. This or all may be gilded or silvered.

Another marine framed in pine has three small ropes
stretched over the frames, weaving in one another at the
corners and securely fastened.

A fishing boat with figures is framed in fine white and
red split bamboo, with an outer rim of fishing-rod bamboo crossing and projecting at the corners.

A hunting scene is framed in plain wood, and for this
purpose Georgia pine, which has rich grain and color, is
good. Across the corners are leather straps and buckles,
or braided leather with tasselled ends hang down the
sides, and are all silvered.

A photograph of some musical subject has a plain,
smooth wood frame, which may be also gilded or silvered. In each corner there is a bridge, over which
wires are stretched.

A moonlight scene has a band of blue plush next a
mat of silvered matting. Then comes a band of blue
plush, and around all a moulded wooden frame silvered.

Photographs of the head of the Madonna, by Carlo

Dolce, are framed similarly, except with black velvet instead of blue.

Tea-chest matting and basket matting are used largely for picture mats, and take gold and silver paint with fine effect.

A Japanese picture has a wide split red and white bamboo mat, on which Japanese colored figures are pasted.

Wood frames on which Japanese metal ornaments are fastened are very rich in effect.

Japanese stuffs make beautiful coverings for frames, especially in écru, red and blue with gold. The stuff is simply laid on in pleats, more or less close together, and tacked on the outer edge, and the pleats arranged to correspond in the lesser distance of the inside. This is work that any woman can easily do.

Large-figured cretonnes and other French upholstery goods are used in the same way. The Morris stamped velveteens also make beautiful coverings for frames. These are better laid plain, except with the necessary fulness at the corners.

Photographs of pictures with women in modern dress are appropriately framed in French upholstery goods. An example is of material of blue ground with large flower in colors. The material is arranged curtain-wise over the frame, and caught back in flat pleats and fastened down flat at the bottom. The fastening should of course be on the reverse side of the frame. This is a striking and appropriate manner of framing pictures in which women and luxurious accessories are the subject.

A picture of Charlotte Corday in prison, for example, is framed with strips of dark oak. On the left side are dark rusty brass representations of hinges, and on the other side another piece, which suggests a lock. Brass pieces cross the corner.   Old bits of brass or iron can be used in this way.

The picture of a soldier in uniform is framed in wood. Across the top is a roll of dark blue or green felt with leather straps, which are brought down on each side of the frame next the glass.   The framing is suggestive of a soldier's equipment.

BAGS AND PILLOWS.

Work Bag.—Take a square of soft satin surah—red, blue, or pink—and round the corners.   Turn in the edges and trim with white lace.   On the wrong side an inch and a half from the sides run a silk braid, matching the tint of the silk, in a circle.   This will leave four rounded points.   Run in the braid twice around a narrow ribbon to draw up, bringing the ribbon through a button-hole on opposite sides.   These bags are especially suitable for delicate work to be brought into the drawing-room.

Large Work Bag.—A bag for large work or where a quantity of materials is used is made by taking a strip of pongee, brown linen, or more expensive materials twenty-seven inches long ; sew up the two edges, leaving a slit in the middle.   Gather up the ends and finish with a bow or tassel.   Put on the bag two large brass or bone rings two inches or more in diameter to keep the contents of the two ends separate.

Grandmother's Work Bag.—A piece of brown satin divided into strips four inches wide.   Make a bag fourteen inches long with these, having sewed in between a strip of cretonne having brown flowers.   These flowers and the other forms have been all previously outlined with tinsel-cord, having in it dark reds and blues. Draw up with a brown satin ribbon.

OPERA-GLASS BAG.—Cut a piece of plush and a piece of silk three inches deeper than the height of the opera glasses and a little more than twice their width ; sew up the ends and one side each separately of the plush and silk. Cut a piece of cardboard the size of the flat bottom of the case of the opera glass. Put this into the bottom of the plush, with the seam in line with the centre of the card. Turn in the ends to make a triangular point, and fasten down. This gives the bottom a box-like shape. Treat the lining in the same fashion, and sew together. Run a draw-string an inch and a half from the top. Insert a ribbon, and bring through button-holed opening at the sides. A monogram in couchings of gilt is attractive.

PARTY BAGS.—Take a strip of pearl-tinted silk fifteen inches long and sixteen inches wide, and make into a bag. Insert a piece of cardboard to protect the back and to keep the silk flat. Draw on it in water colors a group of white and purple asters and their foliage. Face down the top. Insert a draw-string of ribbon of the same color. The bag is intended to hold slippers, fan, handkerchief, and may, of course, be made in other colors, materials, and with other decorations.

DUSTING-CLOTH BAG.—Take a strip of butchers' linen eighteen inches long for the back of the bag. Cut the front five or six inches shorter and both six and a half inches wide. Sew together and bind with ribbon. The extra length in the back is pointed, and fastens over on the front with button and loop. It is swung by ribbons. Before making up, the front is embroidered with some floral design in silks or in outline stitch. As many women do their own nice dusting, a dust-cloth bag is an acceptable present.

Soiled Linen Bag.—Take a piece of tapestry canvas a yard long and twenty inches wide and the width of the canvas. Take another piece three quarters of a yard long, and make a bag of these. The longest piece is fringed out at the end, and hangs over the top, fastening the bag. Under this end, which falls over, tack a little rod of wood. Let the ends project, and point them arrow-shape. Tie ribbons at the end by which to suspend the bag. Amusing designs are painted on these in tapestry colors.

Nursery Linen Bags are made in the same way and ornamented with Kate Greenaway figures in tapestry colors. Embroidery can be used if desired, and especially in outline stitch.

Lawn-Tennis Bag.—Make of gray linen the size to hold the balls. Ornament it with crossed bats done in outline stitch, filling in the racket with net like crossings in outline stitch. Below this indicate the net in the same manner. Embroidery for outdoor articles are more appropriately done in browns.

Game Bag.—Make a bag of heavy gray linen, with the back longer and pointed to lap over the front. Bind the edges with brown braid. On the front outline a design on leather of game or of guns crossed. The head of a pointer is a suitable design. Buy a leather strap to swing it over the shoulder.

Rose-Leaf Bags.—Dry the rose leaves in bouquets, and preserve all the petals of the roses of the rose garden. Make a pale pink, blue, olive, or other tinted silk fourteen inches long and seven inches wide. Make for this an overslip of thin sheer linen, grass cloth, or Swiss. Embroider on this in colored silks a rose with its foliage, some single petals, as if they had fallen. Add in outline stitch some pleasant words, as " Sweets to the sweet."

If pineapple cloth is used, the design can be painted in water colors. Fill the silk sack three quarters full with dried rose petals. Slip the thin sack over it, and tie with a ribbon and bows. This rose-leaf bag is a pleasant gift to the sick, who can keep it near their pillows, when the odor of flowers would be too powerful.

SMALL FIR BAG.—To put on the pillow of an invalid, make a small bag of gray green India silk. Fill half full with the needles, and tie in sack fashion with a ribbon of deeper green tint. A branch of pine in outline stitch with deep green and brown silk is a suitable decoration.

SOFA PILLOWS.—A simple method of making very elegant pillows is by cutting out the figures in lace and working over the white net, following out the lines with tinsel and colored silks, and introducing spangles. These designs are connected by crackle lines of tinsel cord or gold thread couched down. The most elegant materials are used in this way.

PLUSH PILLOW.—Use the proportions of a large pillow in dark green plush. Line it down the open end with Nile green silk. The filling is a square pillow of hair. Above this the plush is tied up in sack fashion with satin ribbon. The ends fall open and reveal the lighter green lining.

LINEN PILLOW COVER.—Large square covers for sofa pillows in much use are made of fine white linen, twenty-seven inches square. Put a row of machine stitching all around the inside three inches from the edge. Cut the edge out in blocks two inches wide, leaving space of two inches. Button-hole the blocks, however, before cutting. Finish with lace an inch wide. An inch inside of the line of stitching on the outer layer cut slashes in groups of two an inch apart, each group separated by two inches, and long enough to admit ribbon two inches wide. Button-hole the edges of the slashes. Make bows of the ribbon in corners.

BROCADED SATIN PILLOW.—Use satins of a solid color, which are the handsomest. Outline the designs in colored silk ; follow the shading of the flowers in silks, and vein the foliage. The effect is very elegant.

SAILOR PILLOW.—Make the pillow of dark blue sateen or plush. Make for the border, in heavy outline stitch with white silk, a linked chain an inch and a half wide. In the centre, also in outline stitch, is an anchor, to which a rope is tied, and one end is carried off and attached to the chain of the border. Suitable for a yachtsman.

HEAD REST.—Make an oblong pillow of bronze satin. Cover it with crackle lines in gilt thread or tinsel cord. Swing by olive ribbons over the back of arm or easy-chair.

CARRIAGE CUSHIONS.—Make square pillows of velours the color of the lining of the carriage. Trim with a cord about the sides, and ornament with an initial or monogram in gold.

BALSAM PILLOWS.—These are made of pongee. Of the narrow width pongee take two pieces nineteen inches square. On one of these embroider, in outline stitch in brown, the line, " Give me of thy balm, O fir tree !" in this manner :

Give me

Of thy

Balm,

O

Fir tree !

Sew these two pieces together, and fill with balsam needles. Those which come from Maine are said to have the most aromatic odor. These pillows are said to be beneficial for those suffering with throat disease.

OBLONG FIR PILLOW.—Make a cylindrical pillow of India silk in terra-cotta tint. Tie around the middle with wide ribbon and double bow.

SOMETHING FOR EVERYBODY.

BABY BLANKETS.—For heavy blankets take the English cider-down flannel or the thick American blanket flannel, which has a thick soft matted pile. Make the blanket about a yard long. Finish with big-patterned Medici lace or Smyrna, and line with pale pink or blue surah.

RIBBON-WORK BLANKET.—Make sprigs of forget-me-nots and rosebuds, as if sprinkled over the surface in ribbon work, with leaves and stems of arrasene. What is known as daisy ribbon is used in these forget-me-nots. Small pieces of pink silk are used in the rosebuds.

ROSE BLANKET.—Embroider in silks a large spray of roses and foliage arranged in crescent-shape. Irregular sprays of flowers ornament the rest of the blanket.

CHERUB BLANKET.—Buy a stamped design with cherubs' heads and wings in groups, and outline with blue silk. Below work, also in outline stitch, " Holy angels guard thy bed," or " Sleep, my pretty one, sleep."

CROSS-STITCH BLANKET.—Cut the blanket a quarter of a yard longer than it is to be when made up. Baste a strip of canvas on one end, and work on it an ornamental sampler pattern in German cross-stitch with blue silk. Turn this over on to the blanket, and it makes a border on one end, after having pulled out the canvas threads. Bind all around with two-inch blue ribbon.

WHITE PLUSH BLANKET.—This makes an elegant baby Afghan. Embroider morning-glories in silks and the words, "Sweet dreams."

SICILIAN BABY AFGHAN.—Cream-white Sicilian silk. Embroider on this in sprays wild roses in silk. Face up with ribbon two or three inches wide.

BABY SPREAD.—Make of linen lawn, with a piece turned at the bottom a quarter of a yard. Hem-stitch and finish with fine Smyrna lace. Embroider in separate flowers all over the spread, and with fine etching silk the delicate filaments of "Love in a mist."

BABY SPREAD of white cashmere. Down the centre is a wide blue ribbon, caught down with stitches of point russe in colored silks. Face around the edge with blue silk ribbon and trim with lace.

BABY BASKET.—Buy an ordinary willow market basket. Line it with colored cambric over cotton batting and an outer cover of sheer soft muslin edged with lace. Stuff the bottom, and lay on it a soft pillow, with a small pillow covered with a pillow-case of fine linen, with drawn work at the edges. This is preferred for very young babies to cribs. The outside of the basket may be gilded and ribbon bows tied on the handles.

PIN CUSHIONS.—It is difficult to tell any one anything new on this score. Cover the cushions with light silks, and make them overlaying covers. Always have something that can be taken off and cleaned.

CONGRESS CANVAS COVER.—Cut a square of congress canvas : hem it up with a row of hem-stitching. Draw threads in group wide enough to admit daisy ribbon. Make five or six of these groups with spaces between. Draw the ribbons through, leaving loops at the corner.

PINEAPPLE COVERS.—Make these with hem-stitched hems, and finish with lace. Outline disks singly and in groups with gold. Wash in faint pink, and outline on this morning-glory in gold, with deeper tints showing the shading. In the same way put nasturtiums on yellow, purple lilies on purple.

TOILET SETS.—These are made in the same way as those indicated for covers. Bottles are covered in the same way, and wide frills with frayed edges are box-pleated, making full ruffs about the stoppers.

TOILET BOTTLES.—These are very handsome covered with white, pink, and other colored plushes, with painted disks and frills in silk, such as are described above.

WORK APRONS.—Coquettish aprons for fancy-work are made of pongee. Take a yard of pongee. Hem it all around with a row of hem-stitching an inch and a half deep. Turn it up washwoman style one third. This makes a pocket for the work. These aprons are embroidered. The most common design is, "A stitch in time saves nine," in old Dutch or English letters. The first clause is on the upper part of the apron, the second on the lower part. Another text is, "Needles and pins. When one is married trouble begins." This is accompanied by a design in outline stitch, in which the husband comes to have a button sewed on. It is a pretty fashion to embroider on the pocket part buttercups, daisies, pansies, or other simple flowers in stiff little rows; the upper part is hemmed down, and a tying ribbon run through.

GRENADINE APRONS.—Short protecting aprons of white grenadine or German canvas are made attractive by hemming with a row of hem-stitching and bands of drawn work. Draw the threads in groups the width of a very narrow ribbon; leave space the same width. Make a band of these threads and spaces an inch and a half wide, and weave ribbons through the drawn threads. In selecting ribbons, take two tints of the same color. Use the deeper tint through the outer threads, and the lighter in the centre. On either side of this, if more work is needed, draw groups of thread, enclosing the stuff an inch and a half wide. Draw in this band perpendicular threads, dividing it into squares.

BANDANA APRONS.—Get the brightest of the colored bandana handkerchiefs. Make a perfectly plain apron with pockets. Turn down the top and run in a bright red or yellow satin ribbon to tie.

TOWEL APRONS.—Take a handsome embroidered towel in color and with long netted fringe. Turn over the top one third, and make a line of stitching in which to run the ribbon to tie.

DAISY APRONS.—Make the apron of congress canvas. Bind it all around with wide satin ribbon, or on the lower end face the width of the ribbon up on the outside. Make daisies of rick-rack braid, and fill in the centres with French knot-stitch in yellow. Arrange these on the satin ribbon at the bottom. Make a pocket of the ribbon, and ornament it with a group of daisies. Shirr the binding at the top, and tie.

MOUCHOIRS.—Take a piece of chamois-skin, or wash-leather, as it is sometimes called, twelve inches wide and eighteen inches long. Double the chamois-skin and add pockets inside six inches wide. Cover the several edges with tinsel cord. On the outside work the word Mouchoir or a monogram with couchings of the tinsel cord. Mouchoirs of this sort are especially suitable for men.

LAVENDER SATIN MOUCHOIR.—Take a square of lavender satin and line with pink satin, putting a layer of cotton batting and the perfume inside. Fold up the three corners and fasten. Leave the fourth open. Tie with satin bow.

Pocket Morchoir.—Take a square of cream-white sicilienne. Line it with pale pink quilted satin. On the inside put pockets of the white sicilienne. Finish with gold cords. Other ornament can of course be added.

Japanese Morchoir.—Take Japanese paper mats or paper napkins. Line them with cotton batting, the glazed side out. Sew the edges together by poking holes and dragging through narrow colored ribbon.

Gentleman's Morchoir.—Make the case of rough brown buckram, but line it most luxuriously, for it is a prevailing fashion to conceal the greatest richness under a rough exterior. On the buckram, which takes paint in a bold style, paint a couple of pipes crossed or crossed tennis rackets. Geometrical figures are good. Flowers are in bad style.

Sachets.—It is premised of every woman that she cannot have more sachets than she can make use of. Dry perfumes are much more agreeable than liquid perfumes, and a little powder in drawers and other receptacles obviates the use of liquid perfumes. There is a fashion in scent powders. At present the most popular perfume is a combination of iris root and violet powder. Iris root in itself is a most agreeable but delicate powder. The best way of using it is to buy it by the pound and mix with it some stronger perfume, such as violet, heliotrope, or whatever perfume each one may prefer, and make it up into a number of sachets, and use that combination alone. In using the powder place it between layers of thin cotton batting. It may be renewed when necessary.

Wall Sachets.—Take a piece of long-haired yellow

plush a half yard long and eight inches wide, and a piece of gay brocaded ribbon six inches wide and of the same length as the plush, and sew them together. Make this into a bag with a piece of silk or satin the size of the two strips when sewed together. Three inches below the top, which must be faced inside for four inches with silk, run a draw-string. Before the string is inserted place inside two pieces of cotton batting, with the sachet powder between. Draw up, swing by yellow ribbons, and ornament with flat loops of the ribbon at one corner. The sachet is intended to hang above a register or against a heated flue.

Round mats of Japanese paper, which come in all colors and with attractive designs, make desirable sachets. Place between the two mats layers of cotton holding the powder, and sew them together just inside the crinkled borders. Add a small bow of satin ribbon in one corner, with an end laid diagonally across the sachet. On this string a date or sentiment can be painted in gold.

LINEN SACHETS.—Take two pieces of colored silk three inches wide and six inches long, and make like a flat pillow. Over this put a case of linen lawn, with both ends fringed, and above the fringe a band of drawn work. Embroider on this in colored silks the name of the sachet —violet, rose, etc., as the case may be.

SACHET SACKS. —Bags of silk, satin, and plush, tied like sacks with ribbons, are used as sachets. Take lemon-colored silk. Cut out a disk of light green silk, a crescent of rose-colored silk. Lay them together and appliqué them on with tinsel cord. Paint or outline in gold on these some floral design. They are beautiful and easily made.

UMBRELLA CASES.—These are of stout twilled gray linen. Cut the back perfectly plain, nine inches wide

at the top, tapering down to four inches at the bottom
and six inches longer than the umbrella. For the outside take another piece six inches shorter than the umbrella, fifteen inches wide at the top, and six inches at
the bottom. Crease these exactly in the middle. On
one half embroider in outline stitch an umbrella fastened
but not rolled up. On the other half embroider two
canes crossed, one plain, the other notched. Stitch this
piece on the back exactly down the two centres, meeting
at the bottom. Put the edges together and bind with
fine twilled braid the color of the embroidery. Lay the
two sides in box pleat, showing the design in the centre
of the pleat. Bind at the top. An additional design,
seen in some cases on the top of the back, is two little
girls; one holds a paper, the other looks up, saying,
" Do it say rain?" Initials or monogram may take the
place of this bit of pleasantry.

NECKTIE CASE.—Take a piece of gray twilled linen
eleven inches wide and a little longer than half the
length of a man's necktie. Cut a piece of silk for lining
the same size. Sew the two together except at one end.
One inch apart down the centre stitch two lines. On
each side slip in pieces of cardboard exactly to fit.
Fasten the end neatly. Inside put across at equal inter-
vals satin ribbon long enough to tie on the outside, and
fasten them down. Under these the neckties are slipped
and kept in place. On the back paint tennis rackets
crossed, in brown and red, or pipes crossed.

SCRAP BASKETS.—The simplest form of scrap basket is
the graceful wicker, rattan, and split straw baskets, ornamented with a large bow and many loops of ribbon.

Woven baskets, cylindrical and bowl-shaped, are
painted with bronze and iridescent paints. The ornament is a large bouquet of artificial flowers, white lilacs,

and, still better, artificial fruits, especially large golden oranges and apples. They are fastened with loops of ribbon that harmonize with the fruit. Do not line scrap baskets. It is difficult to keep the lining from soiling.

MATTING SCRAP BASKETS.—These may be made by adjusting a strip of matting to a round bottom of stiff cardboard. Cut the matting a yard long and a half or three quarters wide. Where the edges are joined fasten the ornament, which is the same as that given above.

BIRCH-BARK SCRAP BASKETS.—Take a suitable strip of birch bark and make a cylindrical basket, such as that described above. Finish the top with wisps of willow tinted red, weaving it in and out through cuts made by an awl. Ornament with ribbon.

WASTE-PAPER KEGS.—Take small wooden kegs. Copper-bronze the hoops, and tie wide satin ribbon with large bow around the centre.

CABINET PANELS.—Panels for small wood cabinets are made by painting pink, red, and yellow roses on tea-chest matting.

WALL HANGINGS for country houses are made by painting flat bamboo shades or matting. They are both cool, and protect the interior from moisture. Hollyhocks, cactus, and boughs of fruit are suitable designs.

LAMP SHADES.—Take alternate strips of ribbon and inserting, and sew them together. Finish each end with a point, and add to it a silk ball of appropriate color or a gilt sequin. Shirr around the top to fit the globe or porcelain shade.

A plain strip of silk the depth of the porcelain shade or globe, made full and shirred at the top and finished with silk fringe or white lace, makes a handsome shade. The bottom of the silk cut in points and faced up adds to the effect.

Pale pink, blue, or other delicately tinted silks are pretty made in this way, with designs in thin water-color washes.

FLUTED-PAPER SHADES.—Take a sheet of colored paper by the centre and crease it together with the hand. This will give those fine lines seen in Japanese shades. As the paper is oblong, it gives a novel shape to the shade.

FLOWER LAMP SHADE.—Make a frame by fitting a tin ring to the globe. Have holes pierced in the tin and attach wires, bending them to the shape desired. Parasol frames are for the present popular. A little dexterity is necessary in fashioning the frames. When made cover them with roses and other flowers made of tissue paper. The making of paper flowers is now carried to great perfection. These paper flowers are simply crowded into the frame, completely covering it. Use only one kind of flower—roses or peonies. Light-tinted papers are much prettier by lamp-light. The shade needs no other finish.

JAPANESE BEAD SHADES.—The beads used are the size of a French pea, and are both opaque and transparent. They must be made on a flaring porcelain shade. About an inch and a half above the bottom of the shade fit a string of beads as close together as possible. Between each bead attach a string threaded with beads and falling two inches below the bottom of the shade. Make another row of beads for a head, fitted with bead fringe in the same way, and fit it to the shade an inch and a half above the first row, or so that the fringe will fall an inch and a half below the first head. At the top of the shade fit two rows of beads for a head, and finish with fringe in the same way. The weight of the beads and the flare of the lamp globe adjust the fringe without any further trouble. These shades in green, rose-color, and brown beads are very beautiful.

SUNFLOWER SHADES.—These are intended to screen the eyes from a lamp not otherwise shaded. Cut the long petals five inches long, two inches wide, tapering to a point. Crinkle these up on a knitting-needle. Gum the petals in thick overlapping rows on to a round piece of cardboard. Fill the centre with yellow and black fringed-out paper. Attach a wire bent over to hook on to the globe to the cardboard. Paste paper neatly over the back.

BLOTTERS.—Whatman's drawing-paper cut into any size desired makes the covers for blotters. There is no effort to make the edges smooth : these are gilded. On the cover is painted broad water-color washes, sprays of daffodils, jonquils, tulips, buttercups, and among these introduce some quotation. Other blotters may have irregular Japanese zigzags in gold, with a spray of flowers in the corner. The blotting leaves are introduced inside, and all is fastened together by holes punched clear through. Strands of gold thread or ribbons are drawn through and are tied on top, making another ornament to the cover.

Beautiful blotters are made by covering two pasteboard leaves for the cover with light brown linen. But first this has a design drawn on—we will say of conventionalized peonies. The flower is put in in thin water-color washes or with the aniline dyes. The forms are defined in outline stitch. In the linen pale yellowish pink tints are admirable for the flower. Line the cover with olive satin. The line of the sewing, which should be a little inside the cover, can be hidden by conchings of gold thread.

More sumptuous blotters still, or we will call them

portfolios, are made in the same way by covering the boards with velvet or plush, and embroidering them with couchings of gold thread.

A package of oblong blotters in colors—red, blue, white, gray—fastened together by punching holes through and tying with a ribbon, are very acceptable. A humorous design in pen and ink adds greatly to the blotter.

Small blotters with covers of the Whatman paper cut in squares and diamonds make dainty presents. The edges are left in irregular notches, and are irregularly marked with gold. Maiden's-hair fern in water colors trails all over the color, and amid it is the title in neat lettering, "Extracts from the Pen." The leaves are fastened with strands of gold thread or silk cords with tasselled ends.

FAYAL-CRASH BLOTTER.—Cover two pieces of cardboard with a piece of fayal crash and line with crimson silk. On the back paint in brown and gilt these words :
"Devise, wit."
"Write, pen."
Add below some gay flower.

PALM BLOTTER. Make the cover of gray linen. Embroider solid palm leaves in deep blue crewel, about an inch and a half apart and at various angles. Line and fill with blotters, as usual.

FANCY CLOCKS.—The small round Waterbury clocks are the occasion of many pretty ornaments for the table. Take a palette, have a hole cut in it large enough to insert the clock. But before it is inserted cover the easel with plush, red or blue, which has been previously ornamented. Japanese zigzags in couchings of gold thread are as pretty as anything else. A bow of ribbon is tied in the thumb-hole. The palette should have a wooden support at the back. The clocks for this purpose cost $1.25.

PLUSH PANEL CLOCK.—An oblong panel twelve inches long by seven wide is covered with plush, on which has first been embroidered a rose spray in arrasene. The clock is inserted in the same way as in the palette given above.

PLAQUE CLOCK.—Take a wooden plaque and cover it with olive plush, on which has been painted a few stocks of yellow Maximilian daisies with flowers. Let some of the foliage be brown and sere. Insert the clock in the midst of the flowers.

LYRE CLOCK.—Have a harp made out of yellow pine. The sides may be covered with plush, but it is easier and the effect is as good to stain the wood black or cherry, or gild and bronze it. Paint on the sides a vine and flowers. Gild or silver the strings, or have these of wire, if you choose. Insert the clock in the base, which should be broad enough to allow the lyre to stand firmly.

VIOLIN AND GUITAR CLOCKS.—These are made in the way described above, the shapes of the instruments only being different.

WHISK-BROOM HOLDER.—Take a square or diamond-shaped wood seven by ten inches. Cover it with plush which has been made ornamental by zigzag lines of gold thread or tinsel cord. Tack across the board a band of ribbon that has been stiffened by a lining of buckram. Have this just loose enough to allow the handle to pass through. Initials or monograms in gold ornament the ribbon appropriately.

BUTCHERS' CUFF HOLDERS.—These woven matting cuffs, bronzed and hung by ribbons, make excellent holders for whisk brooms.

HAND GLASS.—Take a white celluloid hand glass and

ornament with flowers in oil paints. Introduce Burns's lines :

> " O would some power the giftie gie us
> To see oursels as ithers see us."

PEN WIPERS.—Cut pieces of white flannel the size of playing cards. Make two groups of five or six layers. On the top of each put small diamonds cut out of red flannel. A suitable combination is the eight and five of diamonds. These two groups are tacked together at the lower part, as if one was half lying on the other.

BALL PEN WIPER.—Cut out a number of round pieces of flannel four inches in diameter. Pink the edges, button-hole or sew on fancy-colored beads. Fold each piece in halves, then quarters, then eighths. Fasten all the points together. Finish with a bow, and attach to the side of the writing-desk.

CLOVER-LEAF PAPER.—Preserve all four-leaf clovers. Buy fine Irish linen paper. The clover leaves having been thoroughly pressed, are gummed on to the head of each leaf of paper. It is a graceful act to use this paper in writing notes of congratulation, or on birthdays and other anniversaries.

CHURCH CALENDARS.—Have the church calendars printed on white satin ribbon fringed out at each end. The ribbon should be five inches wide. Take a piece of rough cardboard, bevel the edges, and gild them. Paint on it in water colors Easter lilies. The decoration should be on the right-hand side. On the left-hand side attach the calendar with some transparent glue, but do not paste it entirely down. Leave both ends free, pasting near the top.

SHAVING PAPERS.—Take a piece of cardboard five inches long and two and a half inches wide. Cover neatly with white or other colored silk. Paint on this a flower or gilt initials. Attach to it an oblong piece of bolting cloth the same width and eight inches long. Finish it with silk fringe or simply hem it. Paint on this " A clean shave" in ornamental letters. Cut sheets of tissue paper the length of the whole.

PAPER SHAVING CASE.—Cut the shaving papers oblong, and suspend them by a braid of tissue paper crinkled, cut into strips, and braided. On to the outside paper attach a bunch of paper flowers.

LAMP LIGHTERS.—Bunches of lamp lighters made of colored papers are made very attractive by crimping the ends over hair-pins, as is done in the petals of the sunflower lamp shade. The effect is very good.

FOR PHOTOGRAPHS.—Take a piece of écru, brown, and gold Japanese chintz eight inches wide and eleven inches long. Cut two pieces of cardboard a little under eight inches by a little over five inches, using the same chintz as a lining, of course of the same dimensions. Insert these two pieces. This leaves in the centre sufficient space to give a book-like flexibility to the piece which is to act as a cover. Cut two more pieces of cardboard the same size. Inside each with a sharp knife cut away the cardboard, one inch from the outside. Cover this with the same chintz neatly. This makes the frame for the photograph. Fasten the two pieces of cardboard thus treated neatly into the long strip, overstitching the sides and base. Tack the upper part together, leaving room to slip the photographs in. Long strips for a dozen photographs can be made in the same way that will fold up. Tie with a ribbon.

PHOTOGRAPH PORTFOLIO.—Form a cover of two pieces of cardboard covered with stiff brown buckram, such as is used in book-binding. Leave plenty of room in the centre between the two pieces of cardboard, at least an inch and a half. Line with crimson silk. A little orris powder slipped in between is not amiss. On the outside paint the word " Photographs" in letters irregularly arranged in black, white, and gold. Above or below pass a wide crimson satin ribbon. On the reverse side paint a dagger that apparently pierces the ribbon, the point coming out below and the head on the buckram.

WOOD BASKETS.—The woven rattan baskets are gilded or painted. Lambrequins of plush hang from the sides. On these put the motto, " Heap on the wood, the night grows chill," in tinsel cord couched on. Wooden baskets shaped like the woven ones can be treated in the same way.

STRAW WOOD BASKETS.—Get a piece of split straw matting. Cut it into a circle. Bind the edges stoutly, and attach stout handles of straw wound with cord. Gild the whole. Two rows of different colored gilt add to the looks. Double the circle in half. Carry by the handles. Occasionally tremendous straw hats can be found for the same purpose.

STRAW BASKETS.—No matter how homely or common the basket, it may be painted in flat color, gilded or bronzed, elaborately lined with silk or satin. Yellow is the favorite color, and finished for any luxurious purpose by ribbons tied on the handles. The different braids are often painted or gilded in different tints with good effect.

WORK BASKET.—Shallow woven baskets are transformed into the favorite work baskets of the moment by lining them with gay French percales, blue with red, pink and green and olive, and yellow with reds. The stuff is brought over in a full puff on the outside. Inside are the small needle book, thimble cases, and pockets for thread. The handle across the top is ornamented with a flat bow combining the colors of the percale.

STRAW PAPER HOLDER.—Take a piece of flat, straw, flexible matting, such as covers tea chests, thirty-six inches long and eighteen inches wide. Bind all around with ribbon two inches wide ; turn up one end and fasten it down, leaving eighteen inches above as a back. Where fastened bows are placed. The turned-up portion is painted with flowers, and " Papers" put among them in ornamental letters. The papers are stuck through the opening. Ribbons hang the holder on the wall.

WALL BASKET.—Take a hoop, cover it with matting similar to that spoken of above. Fasten a rope with small tacks as a better finish. Cut a crescent of cardboard. Fasten it at a little inclination on the lower side. Gild or bronze the whole, and give the crescent some additional decoration. This is a convenient receptacle for odds and ends.

NEEDLE CASES that are pinned on to a convenient curtain are made of different tints of olive felt mingled with red and olive cut into the form of maple leaves. These are then ornamented with feather stitch in colored silks in such a way as to indicate the veinings of color in an autumn leaf. These are grouped in such a way as to represent a cluster of autumn leaves, and are fastened with a bow of ribbon, as if tied on the branch.

PALM-LEAF WALL POCKET.—Take a piece of cretonne three eighths of a yard wide and long enough to full slightly around a palm-leaf fan. In the centre face it down inside with silk in harmony with the color. Lay it in big box-pleats, and fasten it down, the upper part backward, showing the lining. On the lower part fasten a bow of ribbon, which will conceal the joining. Slip a couple of peacock feathers through.

SILVERED PALM LEAVES.—Tie with a bow of dark

green satin ribbon, fastening a bouquet of artificial snow-balls or white chrysanthemums.

Plaster-of-Paris Figures.—Select such small statu-ettes as Niobe's Son, Tanagra figurines, and works of actual merit. These may be treated by rubbing them over with a little linseed oil, which softens the bold white, and which in time makes them resemble old ivory ; or give them a thin coat of bronze, rubbing them to give unevenness of tint. No more pleasing ornaments can be found for a cabinet.

Plaster-of-Paris Reliefs.—Select copies of good works, such as Donatello's " Mother and Child," or some undoubted work of art ; oil, bronze, or gild them un-evenly ; hang on the wall against some tint that will throw them out, such as red plush, ivory brocaded satin, or any choice bit of stuff.

Waste Match Basket.—Take a piece of gilt wire-cloth five inches wide, eight inches long. Double in the middle. Sew the two sides together. Bind the sides and top with ribbon, fastening the edge with fancy stitches running down into the cloth. On the bottom put a row of tassels made with tinsel thread. Swing by colored ribbon.

Turkey-Tail Quill Ornaments.—Turkey feathers for decorating baskets and wall-pockets are made orna-mental by spotting them with gilt and bronze paint.

Fox-Tail Duster.—Run a wire down the tail as far as you can, and attach the wire to a round handle. Wind the two together with colored ribbons.

Turkey-Wing Duster.—Cut two pieces of olive satin to fit the compact end of the turkey wing. Ornament it with a spider's web in gilt thread. Sew the two pieces together, pink out the edge which overlies the feather or fasten down with fancy stitches.

Egg-Shell Fringe.—Cut off the tops of eggs one third deep. Crochet a fine network of silk in which they may swing. Plant in them fine seeds and grasses, and swing them from brackets and cabinets.

Catsup Jug Vases.—These are either gray or red. Paint them dark green, and ornament with nasturtium flower and leaves.

Liebig-Jar Match Holders.—Gild empty Liebig jars, and trace crackle lines over the gold in Indian red.

Italian Wine Bottles.—These slender-necked receptacles, with the bowls overlaid with straw, are much used for holding a single stalk of jonquil or narcissus. Gild, bronze, or silver them, and hang on the wall or stand as a vase. Oil bottles can be used in the same way.

Watering-Pot Vases.—Paint a mottled gray and ornament with wild roses. Tie a bow of pink and apple-green ribbon on the handle.

Ginger-Jar Lamps.—Have a brass receptacle made to go inside the jar for the oil, and a burner and porcelain shade adjusted. Do not scrub or clean the jar outside or take off the wicker work.

Little Tin Pin Pans.—Have the tinner make little pans two and a half inches in diameter, with flaring rims and handles. Paint inside on the bottom a little landscape or flower. Inside on the rim put this line :

> " Bright as this tin may your future be,
>   Is the wish of the one that gives it to thee."

Tie ribbons on the handles.

Chatelaine.—Make a rosette or round bow of pink satin ribbon ; from this depend four ribbons of unequal lengths. To one attach scissors, to another hang a dainty needle case ; to a third fasten a tiny bag for a thimble, and on the fourth fasten an emery ball.

NURSERY SCRAP BOOK.—Make a book of leaves of gray linen fourteen by twenty-two inches. Bind each leaf with braid. Sew down the centre. Make a cover of buckram. Paint on the back a row of owls on a branch—one holding a book pretending to read, or a row of cats in neckties and collars. Use black and white paint.

RAG BABIES.—Old-fashioned rag dolls in sunbonnets and calico aprons are always desirable.

PARASOL CATCH-ALL.—Take a Japanese parasol and mount it in a wooden block about six inches square. Open it conveniently and fasten it by attaching silk cords or slender brass chains to the handle, where tie a bow of ribbon.

FAN CATCH-ALL.—Take a Japanese fan and remove the rivet. Fasten the outside sticks together. Gather up the ends through the holes with a cord. Weave wide colored ribbons through the sticks. Those fans with fewest sticks serve best for this purpose.

HORN VASE.—Take a cow's horn, or any horn; have it tipped and rimmed with brass. Hang it on the wall with a ribbon to hold a single choice flower.

HAT RACK.—Have the carpenter make a large shield-shaped form. Cover this with crimson plush, or whatever color may be more desirable. Fasten this securely on the reverse side and fasten with brass-headed nails on the sides. Screw on six or eight large hooks for hats and coats. Hang this on the wall. It makes a desirable article in a small hall.

ROLLING-PIN KEY RACK.—Take an ordinary wooden rolling pin. Gild it, silver it; cover it with silk and decorate in water colors, or ornament it in whatever way you desire. Screw in it little brass hooks, and suspend it by ribbon, with bows tied on the handles.

CARD BOXES.—They are oblong, the size of two packs

of cards.   A sliding bottom reveals places for the cards.
On the top, which has a bevelled edge, are two open fans
cut out of white wood.   The edges are notched, and in
each notch is a number.   The fans are variously decorated.   A wooden arrow gilded, set on a pivot on each
fan, points to the numbers.   Between the fans is this line :
" Our doubts are traitors,
        And make us often lose
                The good we oft might win
                        By fearing to attempt."

MOTTOES.

MOTTOES FOR TEA CLOTHS AND TRAY CLOTHS.

" MOCHA's berry from Arabia fine,
    In small fine china cups."
" The cup which cheers, but not inebriates."
" Coffee which makes the politician wise."
" A large, sweet, round, and yellow cake,
    The lovely child of Ceres."
" On shining altars of Japan they raise the silver lamp."
" The vulgar boil, the learned roast, an egg."
" Four-and-twenty blackbirds
    Baked in a pye."
" Feed me with custard and perpetual white broth."
" The fragrant cinnamon, the dusky clove,
    The strength of all the aromatic train."
" The mince pie reigns in realms beyond his own."
" A tea-kettle simmering on the hob."
" Spread thy ambrosial stores, and feast with Jove."
" Who can cloy the hungry edge of appetite
    With base imagination of a feast ?"
" Fair fa your honest sonsie face,
    Great chieftain of the pudding race."
" Drink now the strong beer,
    Cut the white loaf here."

"The piercing cider for the thirsty tongue."
"The fruit on the far side of the edge is the sweetest."
"Good diet, with wisdom, comforteth man."
"Let it serve for table talk."
"Flowing cups pass quickly round,
With no allaying Thames."
"From humble Port to imperial Tokay."
"Appetite comes with eating."
"Eat and drink, and in communion sweet
Quaff immortality."
"Then to the spicy, nut-brown ale."
"Herbs and other country messes
Which the neat-handed Phyllis dresses."
"A dinner lubricates business."
"A dessert without cheese is like beauty wanting an eye."
"Better cheer you may have,
But not with better heart."
"Let good digestion wait on appetite."
"Eat at pleasure, drink by measure."

MOTTOES FOR BUFFET COVERS.

"LET good digestion wait on appetite."
"Mistress of herself, though the china fall."
"Old wine to drink, old friends to trust."
"Various are the tastes of men."
"Drink some wine ere thou go."
"To cookery we owe well-ordered States."
"Dinners of form I vote a bore."
"No useless dish my table crowds."
"Ordered dishes in their courses chime."
"On hospitable thoughts intent."
"Taste after taste upheld with kindliest change."
"Decent cupboard, little plate."
"Keep to old wine and old friends."
"Hold the rolling-pin a sacred trust."
"God bless my soul! no apple-pie!"
"Caput apri defero
Reddens laudes Domino."
"L'ami, de table est variable."
"Hunger is worse than the plague."
"That nourishment which is called supper."

MOTTOES FOR DOYLIES.

"This treasure of an oyster.'

"Blessed pudding."

"Sweets to the sweet."

"Chacun à son gout."

"There is truth in wine."

"It may prove an ox.''

"The sauce to meat is company."

"She brought forth butter
In a lordly dish.''

"Two lovely berries moulded on one stem.''

"Any pretty little tiny kickshaws.''

"All's well that ends well."

"Happy them who take the middle course.''

"A fat, round pasty."

"Hot bag puddings and good apple pyes.''

"Nappy ale, good and stale, in a brown bowle.''

"Quaff immortality.''

"The rare mince pye.''

"The plums stand by."

"Delight in pastry.''

"The gadding vine.''

"Jove's nectar sip.''

SENTIMENT FOR FIR PILLOWS.

"Here lives and murmurs, faintly though it be, the spirit of the pines."

"Come to me, quoth the pine,
I am the giver of honor."

"A dream of the forest.''

"The stuff that dreams are made of.''

"Give me of thy balm, O fir tree."

"A sigh to the past, and a blessing on you.''

FOR WORK APRONS.

"A stitch in time saves nine."

"Needles and pins.
When a man's married trouble begins."

"Get thy spindle and distaff ready,
And God will send the flax."

"How doth the little busy bee
Improve each shining hour.''

" Make hay while the sun shines. "
" She weaves a web of colors gay."
" I don't care what the daisies say,
I'll be married some fine day."

MISCELLANEOUS.

" Sounds and sweet airs that give delight."
" Books, like old friends, should be few and well chosen."
" Give every man thine ear, but few thy voice."
" Praising what is lost
Makes the remembrance dear."
" Take me."
" I know a trick worth two of that ;
Make a note on 't."
" Shall I not take mine ease in mine inn ?"
" Do all the good you can, and say nothing about it."
" Respect the burden."
" Malice toward none, charity toward all."
" North, south, east, west, hame's best."
" To rest the cushion invites."
" For thee, Tobacco, I would do anything but die."
" Life is a short summer—man a flower."
" He touched nothing he did not adorn."
" A pin a day will fetch a groat a year."
" Many a little makes a mickle."
" It is hard for an empty bag to stand upright."
" No sun upon an Easter day,
Was e'er so fine a sight."
" Sands form the mountain, moments make the year."
" Dreams are the children of an idle brain."
" Another day is added to the nap of buried ages."
" To-morrow is a new day."
" Room about her knees for all mankind."
" The gathered treasure of men's thoughts."
" The consecration and the poet's dream."
" The world's a merry world."
" Take me."
" Clean hands, pure heart."
" A friend in need's a friend indeed. "
" Rain or shine."
" Every cloud has a silver lining."
" My clouds all other clouds dispel."

www.ingramcontent.com/pod-product-compliance
Lightning Source LLC
Chambersburg PA
CBHW021528270326
41930CB00008B/1150